MW00694944

SOMEONE I LOVE HAS BEEN ABUSED

Jim Newheiser

Consulting Editor: Dr. Paul Tautges

Help! Someone I Love Has Been Abused

© 2010 by Jim Newheiser

ISBN
Paper: 978-1-63342-006-9
ePub: 978-1-63342-007-6
Kindle: 978-1-63342-008-3

Published by **Shepherd Press**
P.O. Box 24
Wapwallopen, PA 18660

www.shepherdpress.com

All Scripture quotations, unless stated otherwise, are from the English Standard Version (Crossway, 2001)

All rights reserved

No part of this publication may be reproduced, or stored in a retrieval system, or transmitted, in any form or by any means, mechanical, electronic, photocopying, recording or otherwise, without the prior permission of Shepherd Press.

First printed by Day One Publications

Designed by **documen**

CONTENTS

INTRODUCTION

Abuse is a growing problem. In 2007 there were over three million reported cases of child abuse in the United States, involving as many as six million children.[1] Estimates of the number of incidents of domestic violence range from just under a million to several million per year. It is estimated that one in four women has been the victim of domestic violence. While the overwhelming majority of victims are women, there has been a growing awareness of the many cases in which men are also the victims of domestic battering.[2] Similar trends are observed in other Western countries, including Great Britain and Canada.[3] Abuse also touches those who are not directly victimized; for example, children are traumatized when they see their parents fighting. It is estimated that 70 percent of us know of friends and family who have been abused, 30 percent within the past year.[4]

The church is not immune to the problem of abuse. Some come into the church having been converted out of violent backgrounds. Many professing believers struggle with sins of anger which can quickly get out of control. I have seen many cases of abuse both in my pastoral ministry and in cases which have come to the counseling center at which I work.

We had known Sid, Jane, and their two young children for about three years.[5] They were involved in the life of our church and appeared to be a great family. When they asked to meet with me one Saturday morning, I couldn't imagine what the reason could be. I was shocked to learn that for most of their marriage they had been engaging in shouting matches which often ended with Sid beating Jane. No one would ever have imagined that such a sweet couple could have such problems. How could they be helped?

Rob and Lucy were a different story. Rob was a very self-centered, angry man. Lucy seemed fearful and withdrawn. One Sunday Lucy showed up in church with what appeared to be a black eye. On another occasion she went to the emergency room with a broken wrist. Her friends in church suspected that Rob was beating her, but she claimed she was just accident-prone. Then one day, when Rob was watching TV, his five-year-old son got in his way and Rob slugged him in the face, leaving a big welt under his eye. Lucy had finally seen enough. She called her pastor for help. What could he do to help Lucy and her children?

Victims of abuse need help. Thankfully, the all-sufficient Word of God provides the wisdom we need to offer comfort, practical aid, and wisdom to those who are hurting. Because of the limitations of space, we will not be able to cover every aspect of abuse exhaustively in this booklet. However, while we will focus on cases of domestic abuse, the biblical principles discussed will apply to all situations of abuse.

What Is Abuse?

In general, abuse is an improper and harmful treatment of another by one person misusing his or her natural powers, privileges, or advantages.[6]

There are several categories of abuse, including:

» *physical abuse,* which is behavior that results in the non-accidental injury of the victim (who could be a child or an adult);

» *sexual abuse of an adult,* which includes molestation and rape;

» *sexual abuse of a child,* which is any use of a child for the purpose of providing sexual gratification;

» *verbal and emotional abuse,* which includes hateful, threatening, and manipulative speech and actions.

Let's consider a few more examples of various kinds of abuse.

Diane's greatest desire is to be the perfect wife and mother, but sometimes she loses control and spanks her small children in anger, leaving welts. Her husband, Al, doesn't know if he can safely leave his wife at home alone with their children. What can be done to help this family? Does Diane need to be reported to the police?

When Marsha and Craig got married six years ago, they knew it would be a challenge to blend their two families. They never imagined, however, how bad things would get. One morning Craig's twelve-year-old daughter, Naomi, complained that her sixteen-year-old step-brother, Brad, had come into her room the previous night and touched her inappropriately. At first Brad denied doing anything; then he admitted that he had come into her room, but said that he had not touched her. Where do Marsha and Craig go from here?

When Roger and Christine got into an argument, Roger, who is a police officer, took out his revolver and waved it at Christine and the baby and said, "Maybe I'll just shoot you both and then shoot myself. Then all the pain will be over." Later Roger said that he was just being dramatic and that he never intended to hurt anyone. Christine wonders if she needs to report his actions to the authorities, but worries that Roger will lose his job when his employer finds out what he did.

Does the Bible, which was written centuries

ago, have anything to say to people like Al, Diane, Marsha, Craig, Roger, and Christine? God has given us principles in his Word that apply to all people living in every age. In Scripture we have examples of people who were abused. We also have an explanation of why people harm one another in this way. Most importantly, God's Word speaks with compassion and hope to those who have been abused and gives them guidance as to how they can find security in the Lord.

2

A Biblical Understanding of Abuse

While the word "abuse" is rarely used in the Bible, Scripture contains examples of victims of abuse and thoroughly addresses the spiritual issues behind abuse. Joseph, the son of Jacob, was physically and emotionally abused by his brothers, who threw him into a pit to starve to death and then sold him as a slave (Genesis 37:18–28). In the days of the judges, the sexual assault and murder of a woman led to a civil war in Israel (Judges 19:25–ch. 20). Jesus was the victim of horrible verbal and physical abuse leading up to his death (Matthew 27:39), which is one reason why he is able to sympathize with all who have been abused (Hebrews 2:18; 4:15).

It is important that we define "abuse" biblically. Not everything which the world labels "abusive" is evil. For example, some so-called parenting experts claim that all spanking of children is abusive, but the Bible authorizes parents to physically chastise their children. "Folly is bound up in the heart of a child, but the rod of discipline drives it far from him" (Proverbs 22:15). However, spanking can become abusive when an out-of-control parent punishes in vengeful anger and causes injury to the child (Proverbs 25:28; Romans 12:19).[7]

Abuse Can Be Hard to Prove

While all claims of abuse must be taken seriously, accusations of abuse can be difficult to sort out when there are no objective eyewitnesses to corroborate conflicting accounts. Alleged victims often exaggerate or distort the extent of the abuse. In addition to protecting victims from abuse, we must also protect people from being falsely accused. I once listened to a rebellious fifteen-year-old girl threaten to falsely accuse her father of molesting her if he would not give her the greater freedom she demanded. In another case, a woman who was living in a home for recovering addicts had her friend scratch her face and then told the police that one of the workers had done it. We cannot treat someone as guilty without adequate proof (Deuteronomy 19:15; 17:6). Some situations can be perplexing. We pity the police officers who sometimes are called in to mediate in situations

A Biblical Understanding of Abuse

of "he said and she said." Wrong conclusions may be reached because some abusers are very articulate and persuasive, while many victims are afraid to speak out. Situations are further complicated by the fact that there often is significant sin and provocation on both sides. On the other hand, it is wrong to simply assume that both sides are equally to blame.

Don't Rush to Judgment

Before reaching conclusions we must carefully investigate the facts and hear from all sides.

> The one who states his case first
> seems right, until the other comes and
> examines him.
>
>   (Proverbs 18:17;
>   see also 18:13, 15)

Appearances can be deceiving. One night, as I ushered a couple into my office for counseling, I observed that the wife had a black eye. I was gearing myself up for a major forceful confrontation of her husband. When they came into the room I asked the husband, "How did your wife get that black eye?" He replied, "It happened when I threw my cell phone at her." As my righteous anger was rising the wife chimed in, "That was right after I tried to run him over in the car and broke his leg."

Abuse Is Sin

It is important to use biblical language and texts as we seek to understand abuse. Abuse is sin. Jesus labels even verbal abuse as murderous:

> You have heard that it was said to those of old, "You shall not murder; and whoever murders will be liable to judgment."
> But I say to you that everyone who is angry with his brother will be liable to judgment; whoever insults his brother will be liable to the council; and whoever says, "You fool!" will be liable to the hell of fire.
>
> (Matthew 5:21–22;
> see also Ephesians 4:29; Proverbs 11:9)

If angry, insulting words are murderous and subject to God's judgment, how much more evil are acts of physical violence which threaten the safety and health of others!

Why Do People Abuse?

The Bible also explains why people abuse:

> What causes quarrels and what causes
> fights among you? Is it not this, that your
> passions are at war within you? You desire
> and do not have, so you murder. You
> covet and cannot obtain, so you fight and
> quarrel.
>
> (James 4:1–2)

People abuse because they want something so
badly that they are willing to kill (verbally or
physically) if they don't get it. Sid strikes his
wife, Jane, because he demands respect and won't
tolerate her ridicule. Diane explodes in anger at
her small child because she is a perfectionist who
wants peace and quiet so that she can prepare the
family dinner on time. What may confuse some
people is that the object of our desire may not be
wicked (i.e. there is nothing wrong with a woman
wanting to have dinner prepared on time), but
it becomes sinful when we want something so
badly that we are willing to hurt others when we
don't get it. A biblical label for this kind of desire
is "idolatry," which means putting anything or

anyone above God in our affections.

Abusers Have False Beliefs

Abusers believe that they have certain rights, including the right to be angry (and to express their anger) when those rights are violated. In the moment when they are sinfully venting their anger they believe they are acting justly, giving the victim what he or she deserves for certain wrongdoings. By doing this the abuser is (in his or her mind) playing God, taking righteous vengeance upon those who have wronged him or her (Romans 12:19). Instead the abuser should realize that

> the anger of man does not produce the
> righteousness of God.
>
> (James 1:20)

Such sins, however, are not limited to those who are guilty of domestic violence. Each of us will be tempted to become angry and vengeful when others fail to meet our expectations. We may choose to express our anger in more socially acceptable ways such as silent, sullen bitterness, but the root of the sin is the same. We each also need to watch our own hearts, because when wrong desires are conceived in our hearts they may give birth to deadly sinful acts (James 1:14–15).

> A man of wrath stirs up strife, and one
> given to anger causes much transgression.
> (Proverbs 29:22)

There are many marriages in which both husband and wife are guilty of both verbal and physical abuse. Many abusers have the false belief that their abusive behavior is no big deal.

Bart, who is a Marine drill-sergeant, was guilty of frequent verbal outbursts toward his wife, Nancy, and their kids. Nancy was tired of being treated like a wayward recruit and threatened to leave him if he didn't come in for counseling. The counselor asked Bart if he had ever hit Nancy. Bart indignantly said, "Of course not! It is dishonorable for a man to hit a woman." The counselor sought to help Bart see that his hateful words were, in Jesus's view, murderous. Furthermore, if Bart could restrain himself from physically abusing his wife, he was also capable, with God's help, of verbal self-control. The counselor went on to focus on the heart issues, including a lack of grace (see Matthew 18:21–35) which led to anger (Mark 7:20–23).

Abuse May Seem to Get Results

An abuser often continues to practice abuse because, from his or her perspective, it works. An abusive husband often succeeds in getting what he wants, at least in the short term, through intimidation or violence. His wife is constantly walking on eggshells trying to avoid doing anything to set him off again. In her own insecurity, she may believe him when he blames her for his anger. As a result she may make extraordinary efforts to placate him. Yet even if there is outward compliance to his demands, he may sense that he does not have her love and respect. No matter how hard she tries, she cannot fully please him, and so sooner or later he will blow up in anger. In the same way, some parents learn that they can, to some extent, control their children's outward behavior through screaming at them and beating them in anger. Such an approach is not training in godliness and will assuredly provoke their children to imitate their sinful anger (Ephesians 6:4).

Characteristics of Abusers

Abusers lack the fruit of the Holy Spirit, especially self-control (see Galatians 5:22).

> *A man without self-control is like a city*
> *broken into and left without walls.*
> (Proverbs 25:28)

They tend to be proud and self-centered, rather than considering others more important than themselves (Philippians 2:3–4) and sacrificially loving others (Ephesians 5:25–33). While abusers may profess remorse over their behavior, their sorrow is often a worldly sorrow (2 Corinthians 7:10). Even when they are caught in their abusive behavior they are typically more concerned about the consequences of what will happen to them than the harm they have inflicted upon their victims.

Cycles of Abuse

It has been observed that abuse typically follows a cycle:[8]

1. *Build-up stage.* Tension builds as the abuser becomes increasingly irritable, seething with anger.

2. *Blow-up stage.* The abuser loses control and verbally or physically assaults his or her victim(s).

3. *Remorse stage*. The abuser may appear to be deeply troubled by what he or she has done, even crying and pleading for forgiveness.

4. *Build-up stage*. Once the crisis of the blow-up stage has ended and life has returned to "normal," tensions start to rise again.

By God's grace the cycle of abuse can be broken, either as the abuser is humbled and broken before God, or as the victim is helped to find safety.

3

Helping the Victim
of Abuse

The victim of abuse is in desperate need of help. She often doesn't know what to do or where to turn. God, in his Word, has revealed principles she can follow and practical steps she can take. (As most victims of abuse are women, I use "she" to refer to the victim and "he" to refer to the abuser. This is not to deny that, as stated in the Introduction, men are increasingly becoming victims of abuse from women.)

1. She Needs to Be Safe

The Lord is concerned for the weak and oppressed.

> O LORD, you hear the desire of the afflicted;
>   you will strengthen their heart; you will
>   incline your ear
>   to do justice to the fatherless and the
>   oppressed,
>   so that man who is of the earth may strike

terror no more.

(Psalm 10:17–18)

He also calls upon his people to protect those who are in danger.

> Give justice to the weak and the fatherless;
>   maintain the right of the afflicted and the
>   destitute.
> Rescue the weak and the needy;
>   deliver them from the hand of the wicked.
> (Psalm 82:3–4)

> Open your mouth for the mute,
>   for the rights of all who are destitute.
> Open your mouth, judge righteously,
>   defend the rights of the poor and needy.
> (Proverbs 31:8–9)

Those of us who minister to victims of abuse should be ministers of God's compassion for the oppressed as we "weep with those who weep" (Romans 12:15).

A person who is at risk of significant physical harm needs to be protected. This may include having a battered woman and her children live with family members until the situation can be resolved. If the family cannot help, her church may need to provide for her shelter and other basic needs. The civil authorities may need to be called in to arrest the abuser if he has committed a crime, or to deliver a restraining order if the victim believes she continues to be at risk in her new location. In cases of child abuse (physical or sexual), most jurisdictions require pastors and counselors to report the perpetrator to the local child protective agency. When Lucy told her pastor about Rob's violent outburst against their five-year-old, the pastor had no choice but to call Child Protective Services. The police came to Rob's place of work and arrested him. Rob had to undergo anger-management classes and to serve a time of probation, during which he could only have supervised visitation with his kids. When sixteen-year-old Brad molested his twelve-year-old step-sister, Naomi, he had committed a crime and the authorities had to get involved because Naomi needed to be protected.

In cases of domestic conflict, the church should step in to offer counseling and accountability for both the husband and the wife. Rules may be established in advance so that, if either party feels that a situation is becoming unsafe, both parties will go to separate rooms to pray and read the

Scriptures before resuming a conversation which had gotten heated. Practical steps may be taken so that the wife (or husband) can phone a pastor or elder if a situation seems to be getting out of hand. A "safe house" may be made available for when the wife believes that she and her children are in danger. In some cases, when the problem, which has been hidden from anyone outside the home, is exposed and accountability is established, significant progress is made.

2. She Needs to Face Up to Personal Sin

Jesus taught us that we must first deal with our own sins before we can address the sins of others (Matthew 7:1–5).

Most domestic conflicts involve some fault, including physical violence, on both sides. Ed Welch writes, "You should typically expect to find two sinners embroiled with each other, not one irredeemable monster oppressing one innocent victim who needs no redemption."[9] While there is never an excuse for physical abuse, some victims are guilty of verbal assault, being quarrelsome (Proverbs 20:3; 21:9) or deliberately provoking their spouses to anger. When Sid and Jane came to us, Sid quickly confessed that he had been guilty of striking Jane. Jane also admitted that during their arguments she would deliberately "push his buttons" until he would strike her (in her mind, giving her the victory), after which Sid would break down and weep. In addition to Sid needing to repent of his physical abuse, Jane had to repent for her hateful, provocative words. Paul instructs us,

> Let no corrupting talk come out of your
> mouths, but only such as is good for
> building up, as fits the occasion, that it
> may give grace to those who hear.
> (Ephesians 4:29)

We are happy to report that in this case God worked powerfully to grant repentance to both Sid and Jane and that, as church leaders provided them with accountability, there were no further incidents of violence.

While some victims wrongly take all the blame on themselves, it is appropriate for them to make a humble, accurate confession of sin to the abuser. Such humility can be disarming.

> A soft answer turns away wrath,
>   but a harsh word stirs up anger.
> (Proverbs 15:1)

"Please forgive me for provoking you with my harsh, sarcastic words and for not being the helpful, godly wife I should be. I want to work with you to make our marriage better."

It is even more important that the victim confess her own sins to God, remembering God's grace to repentant sinners:

> If we say we have no sin, we deceive
> ourselves, and the truth is not in us. If we
> confess our sins, he is faithful and just to
> forgive us our sins and to cleanse us from
> all unrighteousness.
>
> (1 John 1:8–9)

It may be that you have picked up this booklet but not yet seen yourself as a sinner against God. While it is true that many of us have been hurt by others, it is also true that all of us have sinned against God.

> All we like sheep have gone astray;
>   we have turned—every one—to his own
>   way.
>
> (Isaiah 53:6a)

God's justice demands that our sin be punished,

but he sent his Son into the world to save his people by taking our guilt upon himself and dying on the cross as our substitute. "The LORD has laid on him the iniquity of us all" (Isaiah 53:6b). Jesus Christ has been raised from the dead and now sits at the right hand of God the Father, interceding for his beloved people. The Bible proclaims that

> ... everyone who calls on the name of the Lord will be saved.
>
> (Romans 10:13)

> Believe in the Lord Jesus, and you will be saved.
>
> (Acts 16:31)

By turning to Christ in faith, both the victim and the abuser can find forgiveness and new life in him. Jesus calls out,

> Come to me, all who labor and are heavy laden, and I will give you rest.
>
> (Matthew 11:28)

Sometimes the victim's great sin is that she is more concerned about fearing and pleasing man than honoring God.

> The fear of man lays a snare,
>   but whoever trusts in the LORD is safe.
> (Proverbs 29:25)

A woman who was the victim of "date rape" might have to confess to the Lord that she was guilty of leading the man on or of putting herself into a potentially compromising situation (Deuteronomy 22:23–24).

3. She Needs to Honestly Face the Sinfulness of Others

Many abusers manipulate their victims into thinking that they deserved what they got. There is *never* an excuse for physical, verbal, emotional, or sexual abuse. The victim may need to overcome false guilt. For example, the victim of sexual assault can be comforted by the Old Testament law which stated that the rape victim whose cries could not be heard was innocent (Deuteronomy 22:25–27). Some who have been abused wonder if God caused the abuse to happen because he was angry with them. Yet the Scriptures teach that the Lord is the Defender of the weak and hates those who oppress them.

4. She Must Confront the Abuser

Jesus teaches that, once we have taken the log out of our own eye, we are then free to take the "speck" out of our brother's eye. The abused wife has both the right and the duty to confront her husband's sin (Luke 17:3). If he will not listen to her, or if she cannot safely confront him alone, then others are to be brought in to help confront him (Matthew 18:16). If he professes to be a Christian, it is appropriate to involve church leaders at this point, which can result in public discipline (Matthew 18:17–20). If he will not listen to the church, then he is to be regarded as an unbeliever, in which case the civil authorities may need to be brought in for the wife's protection. A Christian victim who is confronting an abuser who does not profess to be a believer should seek counsel from church leaders as to how to confront him. In cases in which a crime has been committed (i.e. physical or sexual assault), the governing authorities should be called. When a crime has been committed against a child (physical or sexual abuse), the authorities must become involved.

WHY DON'T VICTIMS CONFRONT THEIR ABUSERS?
It is widely believed that the majority of cases

of abuse go unreported. Many suffer in silence, telling no one. Others may tell a family member or close friend, but adamantly oppose confronting the abuser.

1. *Many victims have false guilt.* The wife may say, "It's my fault. I deserve this mistreatment because I am such a bad wife. I keep provoking him by my failures. If I were better, my husband wouldn't beat me." Or "I would feel awful if I caused him to get into trouble and lose his position in the church, or even go to jail."

2. *Many victims live in fear* (see Proverbs 29:25; Jeremiah 17:5–8). Some are more afraid of being alone than being abused. "If I expose his sin he will leave me. I don't want to be alone." Or "If he goes to jail we will be destitute. How will I provide for my children?" Some fear retaliation. "If I report him he might kill me." Or "He said that if I ever tell anyone what he does he will kill himself. I don't want to be responsible for his death!" Some victims are afraid that no one will believe them. "Everybody thinks my husband is a great guy. He is such a smooth talker that he will convince everyone that our problems

are all my fault." A wife needs to trust God by following his Word, rather than leaning on her own understanding (Proverbs 3:5-6).

3. *Many wives have a wrong view of submission.* An abusive husband may twist biblical texts about a wife's duty to submit (Ephesians 5:22-24), forbidding her from confronting his sin or seeking help from outsiders. "I should have a meek and quiet spirit and just take the blame." "If I just submit to the abuse God will protect me." "My husband commanded me not to tell anyone about what goes on in our home. To report him to the church leaders or governing authorities would be rebellious." A wife has the right to physical safety for herself and her children, which includes her right to seek help from those who are appointed by God to protect her.

4. *Some victims are confused.* "It isn't his fault he acts this way. He's mentally ill." "Maybe it's normal for husbands to hit their wives. After all, parents spank their kids. He's usually a nice guy and he always apologizes after he hits me." The Bible offers no excuse for verbal or physical assault (Matthew 5:21-26). These are dangerous sins which can escalate to

deadly levels.

5.   *Some victims don't want to be guilty of sinfully taking revenge on the perpetrator.* While the Bible forbids hateful acts of personal revenge (which means that the victim would be wrong to retaliate by physically assaulting the abuser [Romans 12:19–21]), God has appointed leaders in the government and in the church to enact justice on his behalf Romans 13:4; Matthew 18:19–20).

WHY MUST THE ABUSER BE CONFRONTED?

1.   *For the sake of his own soul.*

> Brothers, if anyone is caught in any transgression, you who are spiritual should restore him in a spirit of gentleness. Keep watch on yourself, lest you too be tempted. Bear one another's burdens, and so fulfill the law of Christ.
> (Galatians 6:1–2)

For the abuser to continue in his pattern of murderous words and actions only further hardens his heart and puts his soul in danger. God may use the accountability that comes with confrontation to bring him to repentance.

2. *For the safety of the victim who has a right to live in safety*. The Lord is deeply concerned about those who are oppressed and has appointed the family, the church, and the government to protect the weak.

3. *For the sake of others who might be abused in the future*. Sometimes the victim of physical abuse or sexual assault would prefer to just avoid having anything else to do with the perpetrator. Sadly, those who abuse, especially sexual predators, often strike more than once. Even if one victim thinks she will never again be victimized, her abuser will probably hurt others. The golden rule compels the victim to do her part to protect future victims (Matthew 7:12). When Roger waved his pistol at his wife and child, he put them in danger of their lives and horribly abused his privileges as a police officer. His actions needed to be reported, both for the safety of his family and because others would be at risk from a man who carried a gun but couldn't control his temper.

4. *If the abuser claims to be a Christian, for the sake of the purity and reputation of Christ's*

church (1 Corinthians 5:1–6; Matthew 18:15–20).
Christ is deeply committed to the holiness of
his church and has established processes of
church discipline so that those committing
scandalous sins can either repent or be
removed from the body of believers.

5. She Needs to Be Prepared to Offer Biblical Forgiveness

The victim of abuse often wonders whether she
is obligated to forgive her abuser, and how such
forgiveness works out in practical terms.

We forgive because we have been forgiven. God's
grace to us in the gospel of Christ both compels us
to forgive and gives us the power by which we are
able to forgive. Paul writes,

> Be kind to one another, tenderhearted,
> forgiving one another, as God in Christ
> forgave you.
>
> (Ephesians 4:32)

Jesus, when asked by his disciples about their
obligation to forgive, told the parable of the servant
who was forgiven a debt of 10,000 talents (the ESV
Study Bible estimates the modern equivalent to

be at least $6 billion[10]). Another servant owed the forgiven servant a debt of 100 denarii, which was still a large sum (about $12,000 in today's measure[11]), but a tiny fraction of the debt which had been forgiven by the master. The servant who had received such great grace showed no mercy on his fellow servant and put him in prison until he could pay the debt. When the master learned of the wickedness of the unmerciful servant he punished him severely. Jesus concluded with the warning,

> So also my heavenly Father will do to
> every one of you, if you do not forgive
> your brother from your heart.
> (Matthew 18:21–35)

If we have been forgiven the infinite debt of our sin and guilt through the payment Jesus made on the cross for us, he expects us to forgive those who wrong us. Not only does his grace compel us to forgive, it also helps us to have the ability to forgive. As we take our eyes off the wrong others have done to us and remember how great our guilt was before God and how Jesus freely bore that guilt for us, we feel compelled to forgive. If you have been abused and are a believer, as terrible as the pain inflicted by your abuser may have been, God's grace to you has been greater and his own Son has suffered more on your behalf. You may ask, "What if I don't feel like forgiving the person who hurt me?" Forgiveness is not primarily a feeling; rather we choose, in loving obedience to God, to grant forgiveness.

Learn to distinguish between worldly sorrow and true repentance. Forgiveness can only be fully granted when the guilty party is repentant. When we discussed the cycle of abuse, we saw that abusers often show temporary remorse for their behavior. Paul warns that not all remorse is godly and sincere:

> godly grief produces a repentance that
> leads to salvation without regret, whereas
> worldly grief produces death.
>
> (2 Corinthians 7:10)

Many abusers are "sorry" because they hate the consequences of the evil they have done, rather than hating their sin. Sometimes they talk as if they are the victims, complaining about how hard their lives have become. They selfishly demand to be forgiven and trusted. Paul teaches that true repentance produces earnestness which zealously seeks to make things right (2 Corinthians 7:11). The truly repentant abuser will be broken over the evil he has done. He will be deeply concerned for his victim (Philippians 2:3–4), including the victim's ongoing safety. Rather than demanding that he be trusted, he will not even fully trust himself and will welcome accountability. Where there is a credible testimony of repentance, forgiveness should be granted and grace should be shown.

Cliff and Diane had been married for just over a year when they had their first big fight. Both were guilty of harsh words, but when Diane pushed him, Cliff slapped her face. Both melted into tears. Cliff immediately got on the phone to their pastor who had done their pre-marital counseling. The pastor and his wife came over. Both Cliff and Diane openly confessed where they had been wrong. Cliff told Diane, "There is no excuse for my striking you. I hate what I did and would rather die than ever again touch you in anger. I want our pastor to keep me accountable, and you have my permission to phone him if you ever sense I am losing control. Will you please forgive me?" She did forgive him. The two couples had a sweet time of fellowship and prayer together. The pastor continued to follow up with both Cliff and Diane, and so far as he knows, there was never another incident like this.

What if the abuser is not repentant? Just as God forgives us only when we confess our sin (1 John 1:8–9), relational forgiveness cannot be fully granted until the guilty party admits his guilt and seeks forgiveness. Many abusers never admit what they have done. Liz remembers being fondled by her uncle when she was in her early teens. At the time she didn't fully understand what he was doing and she was afraid to tell anyone else.[13] Later, after she was married, she and her husband confronted the uncle, who denied everything and accused her of being a troubled girl who made the whole thing up. What can Liz do now? Certainly her relationship with her uncle cannot be restored. Nor, however, does Liz need to become a bitter, hateful person. She can, with God's help, have an attitude of grace in her heart, remembering how God has forgiven her. She can pray that God will bring her uncle to repentance and she can be willing to grant forgiveness if that day ever comes. She also is free to avoid being around her unrepentant uncle.

Tony lost his temper with his disrespectful fourteen-year-old son, Adrian, and slugged him in the face, giving Adrian a bloody nose. The police were called and Tony was removed from the home. A counselor was assigned to help Tony address sins of anger and violence. While Tony claimed that he knew it was wrong that he had hit his son, he went on and on about how Adrian had been provoking him and that "the kid finally got what was coming to him." Tony refused to seek Adrian's forgiveness until Adrian admitted that it was his fault for being disrespectful to his father. Sadly, the counselor concluded that it was not yet appropriate to allow Tony back into the home.

Forgiveness does not necessarily mean the removal of every consequence. If the abuser is truly repentant, he will not demand or expect that every consequence of his evil actions be immediately removed. For example, if he has committed a crime, he may have to suffer the sanctions imposed by the state (Romans 13:1–7). If he is repentant he will accept that he is receiving what he deserves. If the victim feels unsafe, the repentant perpetrator will agree to take whatever measures are necessary for her protection, which may include making agreements that the perpetrator leave the room upon her request and that there be a structure of accountability in place so that she can call for help if a situation seems to be getting out of hand.

6. She Needs Help so that She Will Not Fall into the Typical Sins of Victimhood

Pop psychologists claim that victims of abuse inevitably become defined by their abuse. Some "experts" assert that victims of abuse will likely become abusers. Some celebrities wear their "victim badge" as an excuse for their evil behavior.

Must victims be marked by their abuse for life? While it is understandable that a victim can be adversely affected by what has happened to her, it is not necessary that she become a slave to sins such as anger, bitterness, fear, and excessive self-protection. Christians have the promises of God's Word and the power of the Holy Spirit. Paul writes,

> No temptation has overtaken you that is
> not common to man. God is faithful, and
> he will not let you be tempted beyond
> your ability, but with the temptation he
> will also provide the way of escape ...
> (1 Corinthians 10:13)

Being abused is a very great trial, but God, who controls all things, will not let you be tempted beyond your capacity to endure. As you turn to him, he will help you to endure without falling into sin.

What are some sins to which victims of abuse are especially tempted? Victims of abuse can be tempted to follow the bad examples set by others by becoming angry and abusive themselves, fighting fire with fire (Romans 12:17, 21). Victims often make idols of their own security and safety, which may lead to an inordinate desire to have control or a fear of getting close to others in relationships. Some victims, in trying to avoid future abuse, become man-pleasers, rather than fearing and pleasing the Lord (Proverbs 29:25). Many victims give in to the temptation to harbor bitterness against their abusers (Ephesians 4:31), against those who didn't protect them, and against God. Some abusers may try to relieve their pain through self-indulgence (gluttony or shopping). Others become depressed.

How can victims gain victory? If we are Christians, we are united with Jesus Christ in his death and resurrection, and sin no longer controls us (Romans 6:1–14). Our identity is not "victim," but a new creature in Christ for whom the old things have passed away and new things have come (2 Corinthians 5:17). We are indwelt by the Holy Spirit, who produces his fruit in us, including love, joy, peace, patience, and self-control (Galatians 5:22–24). We don't have to worry or be fearful because we trust God to take care of us as his precious children (Matthew 6:25–34). He will never fail us (Hebrews 13:5). Our chief concern is no longer pleasing men, but pleasing God (Jeremiah 17:5–8). We are able to live by faith rather than by our feelings (2 Corinthians 5:7). Our self-image is determined, not by our outward appearance or our experience, but by the fact that we have been given the perfect righteousness of Christ as a gift from God (Philippians 3:9). We don't have to go to the "broken cisterns" of the world (such as food, substance abuse, or material possessions) to find satisfaction or relief because God himself satisfies our souls (Isaiah 55:1–2). Rather than being bitter, we can be thankful for God's many blessings in our lives (1 Thessalonians 5:18).

4

How Victims Can Become Overcomers

I have never counseled anyone who has suffered more abuse than Joseph, the son of Jacob, suffered. As a young man, Joseph distinguished himself and became the favorite of his father, who gave him the famous "coat of many colors," which made his brothers exceedingly hateful and jealous (Genesis 37:2–4, 11). Joseph's brothers conspired to kill him by throwing him into a pit to starve, even enjoying their lunch in spite of his cries (Genesis 37:18–25a; 42:21). Then they consigned him to a fate almost as bad as death by selling him to slave-traders, thus separating him from his father and from the Promised Land for many years. Joseph did not become embittered, but rather served faithfully, and God was with him. Later, as the indirect result of his brothers' crimes against him, Joseph was falsely accused by his master's wife of sexual assault and was put in prison (Genesis 39). Even there, Joseph was helped by God and was a blessing to those running the prison. After many years, Joseph was taken from prison to interpret the dreams of Pharaoh, after which he was made Prime Minister over all of Egypt. Finally the tables were turned as mighty Joseph confronted his helpless brothers who came to Egypt seeking grain (Genesis 42). This could have been Joseph's opportunity to get even with them for all the evil they had done to him. Instead of taking revenge, however, Joseph forgave and blessed his brothers.

There are many aspects of Joseph's life which parallel the experience of our Lord Jesus Christ. Though he was beloved by his Father, his brethren hated and rejected him (John 1:11). Finally his own people seized, tortured, and killed him. Yet Jesus, like Joseph, was triumphant in his suffering.

Trust in God's Justice

After the death of their father, Jacob, Joseph's brothers feared that Joseph would finally take revenge upon them so they begged him to forgive them (Genesis 50:15–18). Joseph wept and told them, "Do not fear, for am I in the place of God?" (verse 19). Joseph did not deny that his brothers had done much evil against him. Nor did he question whether they deserved to be punished for their evil deeds. As Prime Minister of Egypt Joseph (unlike most victims of abuse) had the power to gain personal vengeance on his tormentors. He refused, however, to take revenge, because to do so would be wrongfully "playing God." He trusted that God himself would deal justly with his brothers. As Paul writes,

> Repay no one evil for evil ... Beloved,
> never avenge yourselves, but leave it
> to the wrath of God, for it is written,
> "Vengeance is mine, I will repay, says
> the Lord."
>
> (Romans 12:17a,19)

Victims of abuse often have to deal with the gnawing sense of unfairness because their abusers don't receive the punishment they deserve. Civil and even church authorities sometimes fail to hold abusers accountable for their sins. Sometimes there is not sufficient evidence to find the perpetrator guilty in a court of law. The victim can find comfort in the fact that our omniscient God has seen what has happened and that, even if human justice fails, the abuser will one day stand before God who renders justice perfectly. Peter speaks of Jesus's example:

> When he was reviled, he did not revile
> in return; when he suffered, he did not
> threaten, but continued entrusting
> himself to him who judges justly.
>
> (1 Peter 2:23)

Jesus even prayed that his Father would forgive those who tormented and killed him (Luke 23:34).

If you have suffered abuse you might wonder, is it wrong to hope that God will punish the one who has hurt you? The Bible teaches us that God's justice is a source of comfort to the oppressed. The psalmist who is troubled by the prosperity of the wicked finds relief in the hope that the Lord will judge them in the end (Psalm 73:3,16–20). The book of Revelation records that the martyrs "cried out with a loud voice, 'O Sovereign Lord, holy and true, how long before you will judge and avenge our blood on those who dwell on the earth?'" (Revelation 6:10). Paul encourages the persecuted Thessalonians, "God considers it just to repay with affliction those who afflict you, and to grant relief to you who are afflicted as well as to us, when the Lord Jesus is revealed from heaven with his mighty angels" (2 Thessalonians 1:6–7).

Trust in God's Sovereignty Even in Your Suffering

As Joseph considered all the evil that his brothers had done to him, he recognized the hidden hand of God at work.

> As for you, you meant evil against me, but God meant it for good, to bring it about that many people should be kept alive, as they are today.
>
> (Genesis 50:20)

By faith Joseph recognized God's good purposes in his years as a slave and a prisoner, and he realized that the end result was worth the suffering. Jesus, like Joseph, suffered according to God's plan so that his people would be delivered, not merely from physical death, but from spiritual death and judgment (Acts 2:23).

Some think they are defending God's honor by claiming that he has nothing to do with human suffering, but in reality they are dishonoring him by denying his sovereign control over all things, thus making him powerless in the face of evil. Scripture teaches that God "works all things according to the counsel of his will" (Ephesians 1:11) and that "we know that for those who love God *all* things work together for good, for those who are called according to his purpose" (Romans 8:28, emphasis added).

In Joseph's case, God's good purposes for his suffering were clear. It was God's plan to deliver his people from famine by bringing them into Egypt where, over a long period of time, they would become a great nation, after which they would re-enter and receive the Promised Land. Joseph, however, didn't fully understand God's plan during the many years of his suffering. In the same way, if you have been abused, you may not understand why God has allowed your present suffering, but you can trust that because he loves you, he would not have allowed your pain unless he had a great purpose in it.

WHY MAY GOD HAVE ALLOWED YOU TO SUFFER?[14]

1. *God uses suffering as a powerful tool to build your character, thus making you more like Christ.* Paul writes,

     ... we rejoice in our sufferings, knowing
     that suffering produces endurance,
     and endurance produces character, and
     character produces hope.

     (Romans 5:3–4)

James reminds us, "Count it all joy, my brothers, when you meet trials of various kinds, for you know that the testing of your faith produces steadfastness. And let steadfastness have its full effect, that you may be perfect and complete, lacking in nothing" (James 1:2–4). The Scriptures teach that even Jesus "learned obedience through what he suffered" (Hebrews 5:8).

2. *God may use your suffering to bring blessing to others.* Just as Joseph's family was delivered from a deadly famine by means of his suffering, so God may use your hardships to bring blessings to others. I have seen children who have been wonderfully influenced to trust God by observing the example of their mother, who found joy in the Lord in the midst of a very hard marriage. Jesus is the supreme example of suffering for the benefit of others.

3. *God may use your suffering to equip you to comfort others when they suffer.* Paul writes,

   Blessed be the God and Father of our
   Lord Jesus Christ, the Father of mercies
   and God of all comfort, who comforts
   us in all our affliction, so that we may

be able to comfort those who are in any
affliction, with the comfort with which we
ourselves are comforted by God.

(2 Corinthians 1:3–4)

Those of us who have suffered most are best equipped to minister to those who are hurting, sincerely weeping with those who weep (Romans 12:15) and pointing the victim to the comfort we can have in union with Christ. Martha suffered for several years in an abusive marriage until finally her husband abandoned her. She does not deny the pain of the abuse and rejection, but she has found joy and strength in the Lord through her trials. Now she is working in her church's counseling center, offering hope and comfort to battered women. The author of Hebrews reminds us that Jesus, because of his suffering, is able to sympathize with us when we suffer:

For we do not have a high priest who
is unable to sympathize with our
weaknesses, but one who in every respect
has been tempted as we are, yet without
sin. Let us then with confidence draw
near to the throne of grace, that we may

receive mercy and find grace to help in
time of need.

(Hebrews 4:15–16)

4. *God may use your suffering to bring glory
to himself.* Peter writes that our endurance
through suffering proves the genuineness of
God's work in us, which will result in "praise
and glory and honor at the revelation of Jesus
Christ" (1 Peter 1:6–7). Jesus, when asked
why a certain man was born blind, explained
that it was not because of the man's sin or
the sins of his parents, but "that the works of
God might be displayed in him" (John 9:1–3).
No event in history has brought greater
glory to God than Jesus's suffering for us.
We who follow him should not be surprised
when we suffer, as if something strange were
happening to us (1 Peter 4:12), but instead
should realize that all who follow Christ
will suffer (2 Timothy 3:12). Many preachers,
missionaries, and ordinary believers have
glorified Christ as they were tortured and
killed for the sake of the gospel. Rather than
being angry with God over our suffering,
we should submit to his sovereign will and
count it a privilege to suffer for his Name's

sake (Philippians 1:29; Acts 5:41). The faith of other believers will be strengthened and God will be glorified when, in the midst of your suffering, you declare with Job, "Though he slay me, I will hope in him" (Job 13:15). I have known victims of abuse who glorify God by their ongoing joyful trust in him.

5. *Your suffering will help you to appreciate more fully the glorious everlasting hope you have in Christ.* Before Joseph began his time of suffering, God gave him dreams which revealed that one day he would be exalted (Genesis 37:5–11). It is likely that Joseph was sustained in his faith by the hope God had revealed through his dreams. As Christians we have a far greater hope and expectation of joyous exaltation than Joseph received in his dreams. We look forward to being with Christ, where we will receive joy and glory which will make us forget our earthly suffering. Paul writes,

For this light momentary affliction is preparing us for an eternal weight of glory beyond all comparison.
(2 Corinthians 4:17)

I consider that the sufferings of this
present time are not worth comparing
with the glory that is to be revealed to us.
                              (Romans 8:18)

Jesus was able to endure the suffering of the cross because of the joy he anticipated in accomplishing his work (Hebrews 12:2). We are promised that one day Jesus will "wipe away every tear" (Revelation 7:17; 21:4). A related spiritual benefit of suffering is that we become less attached to this decaying world, with its trivial pleasures, as we yearn for the perfection of heaven.

Do Good to Those Who Have Hurt You

Joseph didn't merely refrain from taking revenge on his brothers; he actively showed love to them, saying, "'do not fear; I will provide for you and your little ones.' Thus he comforted them and spoke kindly to them" (Genesis 50:21). Paul also challenges us, quoting from Proverbs:

"If your enemy is hungry, feed him; if he
is thirsty, give him something to drink;
for by so doing you will heap burning

coals on his head." *Do not be overcome by
evil, but overcome evil with good.*

(Romans 12:20–21)

Jesus also taught us to love our enemies
(Matthew 5:43–48). God himself is the supreme
example of doing good to those who have done
evil in that, though we were his enemies, he sent
his Son to die for our sins so that we might be
reconciled to him (Romans 5:10).

How can a victim do good to the person who has
abused her? I am not saying that the victim has
to put herself in a place of physical vulnerability.
She can pray for her abuser, that God would show
him mercy, just as Jesus prayed for those who
crucified him (Luke 23:34). If she has to be around
him she can be kind and not hateful, because she
has experienced the mercy and grace of God in her
own life.

CONCLUSION

Psalm 10 reflects the feelings of many victims of abuse: "Why, O LORD, do you stand far away? Why do you hide yourself in times of trouble?" (Psalm 10:1). The psalmist goes on to describe how the wicked oppress the weak:

> The helpless are crushed, sink down,
>   and fall by his might.
> He says in his heart, "God has forgotten,
>   he has hidden his face, he will never see it."
>
> (verses 10–11)

But then the psalmist turns to God:

> Arise, O LORD; O God, lift up your hand;
>   forget not the afflicted.
>
> (verse 12)

In seeking the Lord, the oppressed finds hope.

> O LORD, you hear the desire of the
> afflicted;
>> you will strengthen their heart; you will
>> incline your ear
> to do justice to the fatherless and the
> oppressed,
>> so that man who is of the earth may strike
>> terror no more.
>
> (verses 17–18)

While for the victim of abuse it may seem that no one cares and that God is far away, she can be assured that the Lord is concerned about her suffering and is offended by the evil done against her. She also can be assured that God is just and will deal with oppressors in due time. He will never leave us nor forsake us (Hebrews 13:5).

The victim is assured of God's love in that he has given his Son for her (1 John 4:10). As she draws near to God, she is reminded that she too has been guilty of sin, and she marvels that God has shown mercy to her by putting her guilt upon Christ (Isaiah 53:4–6; 2 Corinthians 5:21). No matter how much she may have suffered, Christ has suffered more (for her). Furthermore, she is comforted by the assurance that, because of what Christ endured, he fully sympathizes with her and personally helps her in her weakness (Hebrews 2:18; 4:15–16). She also has full assurance that the day is coming when "man who is of the earth [will] strike terror no more" (Psalm 10:18). The wicked will be judged, and those who have trusted in Christ will enjoy a glorious existence in a world where there is no sin or danger and where we are in his presence forever.

Personal Application Projects

The following assignments can be given to help the victim of abuse.

1. Make a plan so that you can be safe—carry cell phone and emergency phone numbers, locate a safe house, etc.

2. Make a plan to confront your abuser (see Galatians 6:1; Matthew 18:15–20).

    (a) Prepare what you will say.

    (b) Confess your sin (Matthew 7:5; Proverbs 15:1).

    (c) Confront your abuser in love (Galatians 6:1).

    (d) Bring along a friend if you are concerned for your safety.

3. Learn from Joseph. Read about Joseph's life in Genesis 37–50.

    (a) What parallels exist between what happened to Joseph and what has happened to you?

    (b) How did Joseph overcome the temptation to vengeance and bitterness?

    (c) How was Joseph able to forgive his brothers?

    (d) In what specific ways can you follow Joseph's example in your situation? How can you bless those who have hurt you?

4. Read Psalm 10.

    (a) How does the knowledge of God's omniscience (knowing everything) and justice comfort you?

    (b) Write out your own paraphrase of Psalm 10 in light of your own situation.

5. Read Hebrews 4:14–16.

    (a) Why is Christ fully able to sympathize with you?

    (b) How was his suffering greater than your suffering?

    (c) How is Jesus able to help you in your suffering?

6. Read 1 Peter 2:23–25; 3:18.

    (a) What kinds of abuse did Jesus suffer?

    (b) How did he respond to those who abused him?

    (c) Why did he suffer?

    (d) Have you been reconciled (brought back) to God through repentant faith in Christ?

7.   List some particular temptations you face as a result of what has happened to you and make a plan for how you will overcome them (1 Corinthians 10:13).

8.   We are told that God works all things together for his people's good (Romans 8:28). What are some possible good ways in which God may work through the evil others have done to you? (See also Genesis 50:20.)

9.   Identify a mature (same-gender) friend with whom you can meet regularly for mutual encouragement in the Lord during this difficult period in your life (see Titus 2:3–5). If you find it hard to identify a suitable friend, seek help from your pastor.

Where Can I Get More Help?

Books and Other Publications

Bridges, Jerry, *Trusting God Even When Life Hurts* (Colorado Springs: NavPress, 1988)

Fitzpatrick, Elyse, and Cornish, Carol, "Counseling Women Abused as Children," ch. 14 in *Women Helping Women* (Eugene, OR: Harvest House, 1997), 339–366

Powlison, David, "Predator, Prey, and Protector: Helping Victims Think and Act from Psalm 10," in *The Journal of Biblical Counseling*, 16/3 (Spring 1998)

Pryde, Debi, and Needham, Robert, *What to Do when You Are Abused by Your Husband* (Newberry Springs, CA: Iron Sharpeneth Iron, 2003)

Web Resources

National Association of Nouthetic Counselors, www.nanc.org (for referral to biblical counselors in your area and further resources)

The Institute for Biblical Counseling and Disciples, www.ibcd.org.

End Notes

1 "National Child Abuse Statistics," Childhelp, at: childhelp.org.
2 "Domestic Violence Statistics," Domestic Violence Resource Center, at: dvrc-or.org/domestic/violence/resources/C61/.
3 "UK Statistics on Domestic Violence," at: home.cybergrrl.com/dv/body.html; "Violence against Women in Canada ... by the Numbers," Statistics Canada, at: www42.statcan.gc.ca/smr08/smr08_012-eng.htm.
4 "Domestic Violence Statistics."
5 All names have been changed to protect the identities of those concerned.
6 Paraphrased from Webster's 1928 dictionary.
7 For more instruction on how to properly apply discipline to a child, see Tedd Tripp, Shepherding a Child's Heart (2nd edn.; Wapwallopen, PA: Shepherd Press, 2005).
8 Adapted from Debi Pryde and Robert Needham, What to Do when You Are Abused by Your Husband (Newberry Springs, CA: Iron Sharpeneth Iron, 2003).
9 Edward T. Welch, "How Should You Counsel a Couple in a Case of Domestic Violence?" in Journal of Biblical Counseling, 15/2 (Winter 1997), 53.
10 ESV Study Bible (Wheaton, IL: Crossway, 2008), 1859.
11 Ibid.
12 Stories like this reinforce the need to teach potential victims, especially young children, to "cry out" whenever anyone behaves inappropriately toward them

(Deuteronomy 22:23-24). Because abusers are highly manipulative, children need to be prepared in advance by being told exactly what kind of touching and speaking is unacceptable and what to do (run screaming to Mommy or Daddy) in case of an incident.

13 This list is adapted from Elyse Fitzpatrick and Carol Cornish, "Counseling Women Abused as Children," in Women Helping Women (Eugene, OR: Harvest House, 1997), 351–355.

BOOKS IN THE HELP! SERIES INCLUDE...

(More titles in preparation)